How to use this book

Follow the advice, in italics, given for you on each page.
Support the children as they read the text that is shaded in cream.
Praise *the children at every step!*
Detailed guidance is provided in the Read Write Inc. Phonics Handbook.

9 reading activities
Children:
1 *Practise reading the speed sounds.*
2 *Read the green, red and challenge words for the non-fiction text.*
3 *Listen as you read the introduction.*
4 *Discuss the vocabulary check with you.*
5 *Read the non-fiction text.*
6 *Re-read the non-fiction text and discuss the 'questions to talk about'.*
7 *Re-read the non-fiction text with fluency and expression.*
8 *Answer the questions to 'read and answer'.*
9 *Practise reading the speed words.*

Speed sounds

Consonants Say the pure sounds (do not add 'uh').

f	l	m	n	r	s	v	z	sh	**th**	**ng**
ff	(ll)	mm	nn	rr	ss	ve	zz			nk
			kn	wr			s			

b	c	d	g	h	j	p	qu	t	w	x	y	ch
bb	k	dd	gg			pp		tt	wh			(tch)
	(ck)											

Vowels Say the vowel sound and then the word, eg 'a', 'at'.

at	hen	in	on	up	day	see	high	blow
	head					happy		

zoo	look	car	for	fair	whirl	shout	boy
			door				
			snore				

*Each box contains one sound but sometimes more than one grapheme. Focus graphemes are **circled**.*

Green words

Read in Fred Talk (pure sounds).

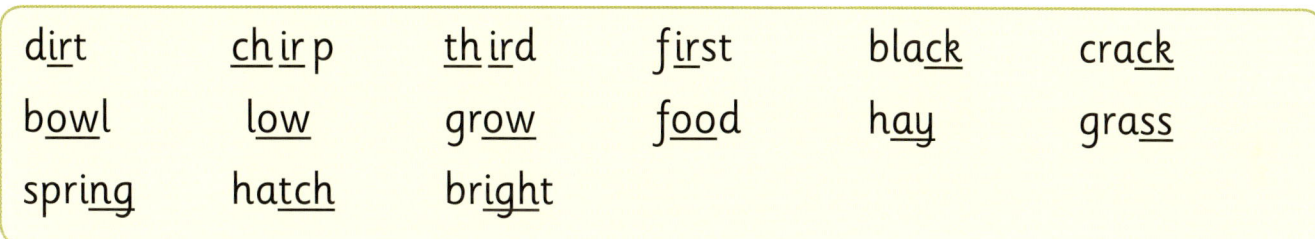

Read in syllables.

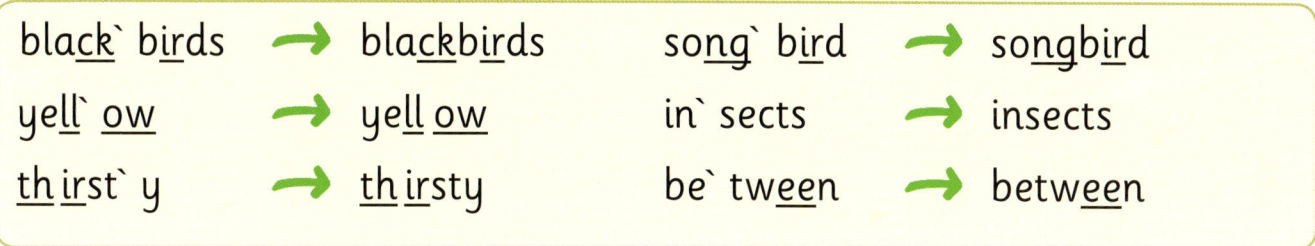

Read the root word first and then with the ending.

peck → pecks	feed → feeds	grub → grubs
drink → drinks	brood → broods	lay → lays
drink → drinking	nest → nesting	

Red words

the   he   water   her   she   they

Challenge words

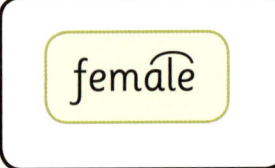

Blackbirds

Introduction

Have you ever seen a blackbird? This book will show you what blackbirds eat and drink, how they build their nests and how they look after their young.

Written by Gill Munton

Vocabulary check

Discuss the meaning (as used in the non-fiction text) after the children have read the word.

	definition
female	an animal or person who can be a mother
brood	a group of birds that hatch together
bill	a bird's beak

Punctuation to note:

The He	Capital letters that start sentences
.	Full stop at the end of each sentence
–	Dash that means the same as the word 'to'

The blackbird is a British songbird. He has a bright yellow bill and black legs and feet.

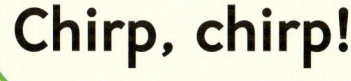

Chirp, chirp!

bill

Food and drink

He pecks at the dirt and feeds on insects and grubs.

When he is thirsty, he drinks water.

This blackbird is drinking from a bowl in a garden.

Nesting

The female blackbird has her nest in a low tree or a bush.

First, she gets hay, grass and twigs for the nest.

Then she puts mud in it too.

The eggs

The female blackbird has 2–3 broods in the spring.

She lays between 3 and 5 eggs.

She sits on them until they hatch.

The chicks

In the third week, the shells crack and the chicks hatch.

The blackbird feeds the chicks until they grow up.

Questions to talk about

Re-read the page. Read the question to the children. Tell them whether it is a FIND IT *question or* PROVE IT *question.*

FIND IT	PROVE IT
✓ Turn to the page	✓ Turn to the page
✓ Read the question	✓ Read the question
✓ Find the answer	✓ Find your evidence
	✓ Explain why

Page 9:	FIND IT	What colour is a blackbird's bill?
Page 11:	FIND IT	What does a blackbird drink?
Page 13:	FIND IT	What does the female blackbird get to make her nest?
Page 14:	FIND IT	How many broods does the blackbird have each spring?
Page 14:	PROVE IT	When does the blackbird lay her eggs?
Page 16:	PROVE IT	How long does it take for her eggs to hatch?

Questions to read and answer

(Children complete without your help.)

1. The blackbird is a British **grub** / **songbird** / **insect**.
2. The female blackbird has her **bowl** / **nest** / **water** in a low tree or bush.
3. She lays between 3 and 5 **twigs** / **eggs** / **nests**.
4. She sits on the eggs until they **lay** / **sing** / **hatch**.
5. The blackbird **feeds** / **nests** / **drinks** the chicks until they grow up.